D1433560

C0000020068479

You Know You're Having a

Midlife Crisis

When...

Mike Haskins & Clive Whichelow
Illustrations by Ian Baker

summersdale

YOU KNOW YOU'RE HAVING A MIDLIFE CRISIS WHEN…

First published in 2009

This edition copyright © Mike Haskins and Clive Whichelow, 2017

Illustrations by Ian Baker

All rights reserved.

No part of this book may be reproduced by any means, nor transmitted, nor translated into a machine language, without the written permission of the publishers.

Mike Haskins and Clive Whichelow have asserted their right to be identified as the authors of this work in accordance with sections 77 and 78 of the Copyright, Designs and Patents Act 1988.

Condition of Sale
This book is sold subject to the condition that it shall not, by way of trade or otherwise, be lent, resold, hired out or otherwise circulated in any form of binding or cover other than that in which it is published and without a similar condition including this condition being imposed on the subsequent publisher.

Summersdale Publishers Ltd
46 West Street
Chichester
West Sussex
PO19 1RP
UK

www.summersdale.com

Printed and bound in China

ISBN: 978-1-78685-019-5

Substantial discounts on bulk quantities of Summersdale books are available to corporations, professional associations and other organisations. For details contact general enquiries: telephone: +44 (0) 1243 771107, fax: +44 (0) 1243 786300 or email: enquiries@summersdale.com.

To...

From..

Introduction

You're not as young as you used to be, you're not as fit as you want to be and you've got a great future behind you. Don't worry; it's only a midlife crisis! There, does that reassure you? No, thought not. The fact is it's all in the mind – at least what's left of it. You've read somewhere that as you get older your brain cells are dropping off the perch at a rate of about 10,000 per day. Plus, your body is going to seed; too much TV, not enough TLC, all jam and no gym. Yes, we know, been there, done that and got the XXXL T-shirt.

And now you're starting to compensate. Better late than never, you think, and you're right. You can tone up that body, do a bit of brain training, buy some nice clothes, 'hang out' at some trendy joints and start feeling good about yourself again.

But... (there's always a 'but' isn't there?) Beware! If you start dressing like a teenager you probably will be hanging out – literally. All those bits you've been covering up for years will be popping out like curious campers peeking from a misshapen tent.

And is it really necessary to go out and buy a 500-cc motorbike or a pink sports car and roar around the town like a haggard Hell's Angel or a latter-day Lady Penelope?

You want to keep the years at bay, but with a bit of dignity, decorum and lashings of fun along the way. Reading this book may save you from embarrassment, humiliation and foolishness, but mainly it will save you from yourself.

Don't continue your midlife crisis without it!

Telltale Signs You're Having a Midlife Crisis

You start wearing
skimpy swimwear, even
though you no longer have a
skimpy body to go with it

You studiously avoid socialising with anyone over 40

You start looking for sexier, more exciting replacements for the following: your car, your partner, your hormones...

All your clothes are now made of leather... including your pyjamas

You look like you're auditioning for a lead role in a production of *Grease* that's being staged in a retirement home

A Midlife Crisis is...

... wanting to be less
of a role model and more
of a supermodel

... living it up without being
able to live it down

... wanting to have it large but
not wanting to get any larger

... believing you're still more
hip-hop than hip op

Myths About Midlife Crises

They are based on irrational fears
– what's irrational about looking
in the mirror and being horrified
to see one of your parents?

No one else knows you are going through one – who else would dye their hair bright orange and buy trousers so tight that they can barely get them on?

Your attempts to look younger will make you look ridiculous – the natural process of getting older will probably make you look ridiculous as well... just in a different way

You will never be able to re-capture your youth – you might if you hunt him/her down in your brand new, super-fast sports car

It's a natural part of getting older – what's natural about dyed hair, tummy tucks and facelifts?

Conversing With Others (What They Say and What You Hear)

'You're looking really good.' =
'My God! It must have
cost you thousands.'

'Miserable weather we're having.' = 'It must be playing merry hell with your arthritis.'

'You seem to have plenty of energy.' = 'You're on some form of medication, aren't you?'

'So you're getting out and enjoying yourself a lot these days?' = 'You're going to give yourself a heart attack.'

'So how old is your boyfriend/girlfriend?'
= 'I wish to establish that they are young enough to be your son/daughter before passing this information on to everyone you know.'

Conversing With Others (What You Say and What They Hear)

'I'll just have the soup please.' =
'I can't chew anything at my age.'

'Hello' = 'Hello, I am a young person – honest!'

'This phone line's a bit faint.' = 'I'm as deaf as a post.'

'Would you like a dance?' = 'I need someone to help hold me up.'

To a 20-year-old of the opposite sex: 'Hi, what do you say to going out on a date?' = 'Do you have any objection to me spending my entire life savings on you over the next two months?'

Things That Could Provoke a Midlife Crisis

After running for a bus, you find you need a couple of days to recover

You get more enjoyment out of a box of chocolates than you do from the person who gave them to you

You try to recall all those wild sex and drugs orgies you had in your youth and realise you forgot to have any

You see a photo of Bradley Cooper/ Jennifer Lopez with a younger partner and think, 'If whippersnappers like them can get away with it, so can I!'

Your Natural Enemies Will Now Be...

Anyone who reminds
you of your age

People who just assume that
you're a grandparent

People who are older than
you but manage to look at
least five years younger

Anyone who fails to tell you how great you're looking... for your age

Friends who are counting down the years until you receive your bus pass

Weekly Highlights During Your Midlife Crisis

Successfully squeezing yourself
into those jeans you used
to wear 20 years ago

Starting yet another new wonder diet

Chatting up that nice assistant in the chemist when you go to pick up your prescription of hormone replacement drugs or Viagra

Chat-up Lines You Can Use as a Mid-lifer

'Would you like to see my pension projection?'

'They say the finest wines are in the oldest bottles – fancy a vintage tipple?'

'Don't tell me you'd turn down an opportunity to help the aged?'

'Go out with me and I'll be able to help you with your history homework.'

Your New Outlook on Life

Maturity is overrated –
let's have some fun!

Stand out from the crowd –
just because everyone else
your age is old, doesn't mean
you have to be as well

Having the body of a 20-year-old
is not impossible – it just
may not be your own!

You only live once – but who says
you can't be a teenager twice?!

Hairstyles and Accessories for the Mid-lifer (for Him)

Ponytail – the implication presumably having something to do with stallions?

Odd, spiky haircut – that looks as though a hedgehog has been run over on your head

Plenty of bling –
more than a gangsta rapper
and Mr T combined

The completely bald look – which you hope others will assume you've adopted out of choice

A Ferrari key fob – regardless of what car you actually drive

Hairstyles and Accessories for the Mid-lifer (for Her)

Bleached blonde hair – so bright that people can still find you in the nightclub during a power cut

A thick mane of glossy, youthful and healthy hair – and not only that, it's machine washable too!

The bright red, yellow and green spiky hairdo – or, as it's better known, the menopausal parrot

A loosely worn belt –
so it fools people into thinking
you have a girlish figure

'Sexy' black tights – to hide
those varicose veins

Your Life Will Now Consist of...

... lying about your age,
unless it gets you cheaper
car insurance.

... increasing body maintenance
with diminishing returns.

... trying to get rid of, undo, recycle or get a refund on every bit of rubbish you have accumulated in your life over the past 25 years... starting with your partner.

... acting as a full-time, unpaid human guinea pig for every anti-ageing product on the market.

... telling everyone about the *real* you (because no matter how long they've known you, none of them seem to have encountered this youthful character before).

The Car of the Male Mid-lifer

One that approaches 60 even
quicker than you are

Open-topped – that lets
you feel the wind blowing
through your hairpiece

Satnav – despite your best efforts this may be the only sexy female voice regularly heard in your car

Bucket seats – always handy if you get caught short on a long journey

Plenty of horsepower – just like you, you old stallion

The Car of the Female Mid-lifer

Special in-car shoe wardrobe –
that is why they call it the boot isn't it?

Bright pink bodywork – yes, even your
car blushes to be seen out with you

One that breaks down with surprising regularity so some young, hunky mechanic can come to your rescue

Secret compartment – to hide your driving glasses the moment you stop

Satnav – with a deep, sexy male voice that you can imagine is giving you directions back to his place

Ideal Gifts for the Mid-lifer

A distorting mirror that makes you look permanently thinner

The services of your own personal body/stunt double to save you overexerting yourself at moments of excitement

Clothes with smaller
size labels stitched in

A Dorian Gray-like portrait of
yourself to keep in the attic

A speak-your-weight
machine that lies

Things the Mid-lifer Fears Most

Mirrors in brightly lit
changing rooms

Being seen with any
contemporaries who have made
no attempt whatsoever to hide
their state of advanced decay

Old photographs of you coming
to light that prove you were alive
some decades prior to what
you've previously claimed

Ways You Might Reinvent Yourself

As a sex guru now ready and willing to share your lifetime's erotic experience with the younger generation

As an 85-year-old who has worn exceptionally well

As a colourful character, although not just because you have developed high blood pressure

As a living legend… or, failing that, just living!

As an artists' model, so people will have to look at your flabby body whether they like it or not

New Hobbies You Can Consider

Etching – so you can invite unsuspecting young people back to see your work

Leatherwork – that's what you'll call getting dressed in the morning

Travelling – you'll have no choice;
everyone within a 50-mile radius
will know far too much about you

Rambling – and perhaps
dribbling too

Needlework – or DIY plastic
surgery as it's otherwise known

Pottery – a potter in the garden
followed by a potter round the shops

Music You Might Have Started Listening to

Rap music with offensive lyrics that your parents wouldn't like

High-energy dance music to try to get your heart rate back to what it was 20 years ago

Sultry, sexy soul music to try to get some other parts working

Ways You Now Describe Your Age

The wrong side of 30

In the prime of life

Experienced

Twenty-one again

Ways You Now Measure Out the Rest of Your Life

By the length of time between
your Botox injections

By the length of time it takes your successive partners to get too old for you to be interested in them any more

In hip replacements

Things You Won't Admit to

The terrifying amount
you are shelling out to
maintain your lifestyle

It's only because of Viagra your
body remains vertical at all

That your supermarket trolley is a very welcome means of support

That you look a bit
daft in clothing meant for
someone 20 years younger

Having grown-up children,
let alone grandchildren

Other Names for a Midlife Crisis

A sudden late surge of hormones...
Yeah, right! From the chemist!

'Adultlescence'

The second age… or is it the fifth or sixth?

Getting back in touch with your inner teenager

A few last wishes at the
fountain of youth

Singles' night in the
last-chance saloon

How to Deny You're Having a Midlife Crisis

'I have to wear leather
trousers because I'm allergic
to all other fabrics.'

'No, I've not had any cosmetic surgery on my face. It just looks stretched because, being so full of youthful energy, I ran all the way here.'

'If the fact that I'm bored, I hate my job and I've lost interest in sex with my partner means I'm having a midlife crisis, then I've been having one since I was in my twenties!'

'No, it's not a midlife crisis. It's just that I've been so busy I've only recently managed to fit in becoming an adolescent.'

'My friend was having a midlife crisis so I'm faking one to make them feel better about it.'

Looking on the Bright Side of Your Midlife Crisis

It sure beats an old-age crisis!

At last! You now have something to blame all your daftest behaviour on

Yes, trying to revert to a teenage lifestyle may be futile but, on the other hand, why act like a grown-up when you know you haven't really matured since you were 17?

You get to buy yourself a Harley-Davidson and/or start going out with someone who has one

It's Mother Nature's way of
saying 'Enjoy yourself!'

If you're interested in finding out more about our books, find us on Facebook at **Summersdale Publishers** and follow us on Twitter at **@Summersdale**.

www.summersdale.com